Preparing for your interview workbook.

100 midwifery questions plus more.

Jade Deverill

on behalf of Midwifery & Nursing Online

ISBN: 1482630575

ISBN-13: 978-1482630572

DEDICATION

To all the aspiring midwives out there who work so very hard to gain that place at university. Hopefully this will be a helping hand.

CONTENTS

1 INTRODUCTION

A common question which I come across is what will they ask me at interview? The answer to that is I simply don't know. Each university will have their own bank of questions to use and they may use different sets of questions that they alternate between interview days. Likewise all their maths and literacy tests will vary slightly.

Contained within this book is a bank of real midwifery questions that you may be asked, example literacy tests and mathematics questions.

Using this workbook you can practice with examples of questions you may face, noting your answers within the book to ease keeping everything in one place for revision.

2 QUESTION BANK

These questions have been provided anonymously, as in I won't notify you of which universities they were asked at. This is to avoid disadvantaging others who have had interviews. Use the questions to get you thinking and researching, it's not worth trying to remember all 100 questions and your perfect answer as its just too much work, you also don't want your answers to feel rehearsed.

Using the space provided for each question, write down instant keywords which spring to mind and then from that try to formulate a usable answer. The keywords will hopefully act as prompts to help you remember where to start with your answer when you are under pressure in your interview.

1.   What is the difference between a Nurse and a Midwife?

Keywords:

....
....
....

Answer:

....
....
....

2.   What is your understanding of the role of the Midwife?

Keywords:

....
....
....

Answer:

....
....
....

3.   How do you deal with conflict?

Keywords:

....

....

....

Answer:

....

....

....

4.   Current issues affecting midwifery?

Keywords:

....

....

....

Answer:

....

....

....

5.   How would you de-stress?

Keywords:

....

....

....

Answer:

....

....

....

6.   What would you do if your are not successful this time?

Keywords:

....

....

....

Answer:

....

....

....

7.   How would you deal with a woman wanting a late termination?

Keywords:

....

....

....

Answer:

....

....

....

8.   Why should we choose you?

Keywords:

....

....

....

Answer:

....

....

....

9. If you had a woman that was high risk, but was insistent on having a home birth what would you do?

Keywords:

....

....

....

Answer:

....

....

....

10. Why a midwife?

Keywords:

....

....

....

Answer:

....

....

....

11.   What does Advocacy mean in relation to midwifery?

Keywords:

....

....

....

Answer:

....

....

....

12.   What are you plans for the next few years?

Keywords:

....

....

....

Answer:

....

....

....

13.   Can you mention something that has been in the news recently?

Keywords:

....

....

....

Answer:

....

....

....

14.   What do you think happens in a "normal" labour?

Keywords:

....

....

....

Answer:

....

....

....

15.   What does a midwife do?

Keywords:

....
....
....

Answer:

....
....
....

16.   How do you think you will cope with shift work?

Keywords:

....
....
....

Answer:

....
....
....

17.   Do you have supportive family?

Keywords:

....

....

....

Answer:

....

....

....

18.   Why do you think you will make a good midwife?

Keywords:

....

....

....

Answer:

....

....

....

19.   What would you do if your mentor shouted at you in the middle of the ward in front of everyone?

Keywords:

....
....
....

Answer:

....
....
....

20.   A woman has had test results which show the baby has a condition that is not compatible with life....she asks you what to do...what do you say to her?

Keywords:

....
....
....

Answer:

....
....
....

21.   What have you done to prepare for this interview?

Keywords:

....
....
....

Answer:

....
....
....

22.   What do you understand by the term professional/professionalism?

Keywords:

....
....
....

Answer:

....
....
....

23. What do you think you would find the hardest about clinical placement?

Keywords:

....

....

....

Answer:

....

....

....

24. What do you think makes up a Midwives 'normal' day-to-day role?

Keywords:

....

....

....

Answer:

....

....

....

25.   What event made you want to be a midwife?

Keywords:

....
....
....

Answer:

....
....
....

26.   Why do you think some women don't get good care?

Keywords:

....
....
....

Answer:

....
....
....

27. When was a time that you dealt with a difficult situation? What did you learn?

Keywords:

....

....

....

Answer:

....

....

....

28. What skills and qualities make a good midwife? Which is most important in your opinion?

Keywords:

....

....

....

Answer:

....

....

....

29.   Tell me about your work experience, what insight did it give you into the profession?

Keywords:

....

....

....

Answer:

....

....

....

30.   What is the biggest advance in midwifery in the last thirty years?

Keywords:

....

....

....

Answer:

....

....

....

31.   Should men be allowed to be midwives?

Keywords:

....
....
....

Answer:

....
....
....

32.   How would you feel in difficult situations such as a full term baby
       dying?

Keywords:

....
....
....

Answer:

....
....
....

33. What ways do you prefer to learn?

Keywords:

....

....

....

Answer:

....

....

....

34. What strengths do you have which will help you in your role as a midwife?

Keywords:

....

....

....

Answer:

....

....

....

35. What weaknesses do you have which you think you will need to overcome/work on?

Keywords:

....
....
....

Answer:

....
....
....

36. What do you think will be the biggest challenge in taking on the midwifery course?

Keywords:

....
....
....

Answer:

....
....
....

37.   What is the last thing you read about midwifery?

Keywords:

....

....

....

Answer:

....

....

....

38.   What is the NMC and what do they do?

Keywords:

....

....

....

Answer:

....

....

....

39.   What do you think will be the best thing about being a midwife? And the worst thing?

Keywords:

....
....
....

Answer:

....
....
....

40.   What are the priorities of a woman in labour?

Keywords:

....
....
....

Answer:

....
....
....

41. Long ago doctors helped women give birth, so what is the use of midwives now?

Keywords:

....

....

....

Answer:

....

....

....

42. What were your pre-conceived ideas of what Midwifery would be like?

Keywords:

....

....

....

Answer:

....

....

....

43.   Why have you applied to this university?

Keywords:

....
....
....

Answer:

....
....
....

44.   How will you cope with the demands of university work and clinical placements?

Keywords:

....
....
....

Answer:

....
....
....

45. If a woman made a decision about her care which you thought put her or her baby at risk, how would you react?

Keywords:

....

....

....

Answer:

....

....

....

46. What does a community/hospital midwife do?

Keywords:

....

....

....

Answer:

....

....

....

47.   How does your past employment relate to midwifery?

Keywords:

....

....

....

Answer:

....

....

....

48.   How would you deal with women from a different culture or social class?

Keywords:

....

....

....

Answer:

....

....

....

49.   Where do you see yourself in five years time?

Keywords:

....

....

....

Answer:

....

....

....

50.   What does your family think of you applying to university?

Keywords:

....

....

....

Answer:

....

....

....

51.   What are the advantages of teamwork?

Keywords:

....

....

....

Answer:

....

....

....

52.   What can get in the way of a team running smoothly?

Keywords:

....

....

....

Answer:

....

....

....

53. If I asked a friend to describe you and your strengths and weaknesses and why you would make a good midwife, what would they say?

Keywords:

....
....
....

Answer:

....
....
....

54. What skills do you think you have which would be transferable to midwifery?

Keywords:

....
....
....

Answer:

....
....
....

55.   How are you with time management?

Keywords:

....
....
....

Answer:

....
....
....

56.   What role do you see the male or birthing partner playing in the birth process?

Keywords:

....
....
....

Answer:

....
....
....

57.   How do you feel about antenatal education?

Keywords:

....
....
....

Answer:

....
....
....

58.   Do you feel that those who are already mothers make the best
       midwives?

Keywords:

....
....
....

Answer:

....
....
....

59.   What would you say care means, and how does it differ for nurses?

Keywords:

....

....

....

Answer:

....

....

....

60.   If you could not do an essay, what would you do?

Keywords:

....

....

....

Answer:

....

....

....

61.   What do you understand about midwifery and women's health issues?

Keywords:

....
....
....

Answer:

....
....
....

62.   What support network/coping strategies do you think that you could utilise/or would need?

Keywords:

....
....
....

Answer:

....
....
....

63.   What is health promotion?

Keywords:

....
....
....

Answer:

....
....
....

64.   What values should a midwife have?

Keywords:

....
....
....

Answer:

....
....
....

65.   What would you like to do after qualifying?

Keywords:

....

....

....

Answer:

....

....

....

66.   Do you see yourself as a leader?

Keywords:

....

....

....

Answer:

....

....

....

67.   What kind of midwife do you think you would make?

Keywords:

....

....

....

Answer:

....

....

....

68.   What is your opinion on how the press portray midwifery?

Keywords:

....

....

....

Answer:

....

....

....

69.   How have your A levels helped you prepare for a midwifery degree?

Keywords:

....

....

....

Answer:

....

....

....

70.   If you were given an assignment to be handed in four weeks time, how would you prepare for it?

Keywords:

....

....

....

Answer:

....

....

....

71.   What is your view on home birth/water birth?

Keywords:

....
....
....

Answer:

....
....
....

72.   What role does a midwife play in health promotion?

Keywords:

....
....
....

Answer:

....
....
....

73. You are with a woman in labour, and her birthing partner is being extremely disruptive and unhelpful – what would you, as the woman's advocate do?

Keywords:

....
....
....

Answer:

....
....
....

74. How do you deal with aggression?

Keywords:

....
....
....

Answer:

....
....
....

75.   Describe your feelings about midwifery in one word?

Keywords:

....

....

....

Answer:

....

....

....

76.   What is something you have done that has made you proud?

Keywords:

....

....

....

Answer:

....

....

....

77.   How would you feel about performing intimate examinations?

Keywords:

....

....

....

Answer:

....

....

....

78.   How would you behave if you did badly in an essay you had really
       worked for?

Keywords:

....

....

....

Answer:

....

....

....

79.   What are the dark sides of midwifery?

Keywords:

....

....

....

Answer:

....

....

....

80.   How would it change your life if you gained a place on the course?

Keywords:

....

....

....

Answer:

....

....

....

81.   What would you do after training if you could not get a job?

Keywords:

....

....

....

Answer:

....

....

....

82.   Do you think your lack of a childbirth experience could be a disadvantage in any way?

Keywords:

....

....

....

Answer:

....

....

....

83.   Tell me some of the subjects you will study and why they are
       relevant?

Keywords:

....

....

....

Answer:

....

....

....

84.   Why do you think midwives need a degree?

Keywords:

....

....

....

Answer:

....

....

....

85.   How would you feel about the responsibility once qualified?

Keywords:

....

....

....

Answer:

....

....

....

86.   How would you deal with bodily fluids and unpleasant situations?

Keywords:

....

....

....

Answer:

....

....

....

87.   How do you approach assignments?

Keywords:

....

....

....

Answer:

....

....

....

88.   How would you deal with a mother who is a drug abuser and has come to see you with her second baby (first taken away by social services)?

Keywords:

....

....

....

Answer:

....

....

....

89.   How has midwifery changed throughout the years?

Keywords:

....

....

....

Answer:

....

....

....

90.   In your opinion is sending women home 6 hours after birth a good
       thing?

Keywords:

....

....

....

Answer:

....

....

....

91.   What is Empathy? also Give and example of it.

Keywords:

....

....

....

Answer:

....

....

....

92.   How do you cope with change?

Keywords:

....

....

....

Answer:

....

....

....

93.   What does non judgemental care mean to you?

Keywords:

....
....
....

Answer:

....
....
....

94.   How would you feel caring for a woman having a TOP because the baby had only one arm?

Keywords:

....
....
....

Answer:

....
....
....

95. Give an example of including someone's culture/religion in your care.

Keywords:

....
....
....

Answer:

....
....
....

96. How would you life change in order to do the course?

Keywords:

....
....
....

Answer:

....
....
....

97.   What is diversity?

Keywords:

....
....
....

Answer:

....
....
....

98.   A mother is 7 months pregnant, you have seen her through her
        whole pregnancy. You have to cancel an antenatal appointment,
        and when you next see her the heart beat cannot be heard. How
        would you feel?

Keywords:

....
....
....

Answer:

....
....
....

99.   If you were presented with a dying lady who is a Jehovah witness refusing blood products, what would you do?

Keywords:

....

....

....

Answer:

....

....

....

100.   Which birth positions have you witnessed?

Keywords:

....

....

....

Answer:

....

....

....

3 QUESTIONS TO ASK THE INTERVIEWERS

It's not uncommon for the interviewers at the end of an interview to ask if you have any questions. It's always good to have some questions prepared that you can ask, rather than looking a bit blank or stumped that they've asked if you have any questions. Many people can get caught out by this and get all flustered, if you have nothing to ask then just say that they've covered everything within the day.

Questions for you to ask the interviewers:

1. I've applied to two other universities. If I'm lucky enough to be accepted by all three, why should I choose this one?

2. What are the further training opportunities in the Trust?

3. How many course lecturers are currently practising as midwives?

4. What is the drop out rate for the course? And what are the common reasons for people leaving?

5. How many of last years third year students received jobs after they qualified?

6. Could you tell me a little about the dissertation/Research and the viva module in third year?

7. How is the university and the staff involved in research in the area of midwifery and the maternity services? Nationwide/local research?

8. Is there anything else you can suggest I should read up on/would interest me between now and when the course is due to start?

9. What qualities as a university do you have compared to others?

10. Do you offer case loading?

11. What support is in place for situations such as stillbirth?

12. Do you do problem based learning?

13. There is a lot of speculation in the industry about students being bullied by their mentors during placements. have you ever heard of this at this university? And how would you support your students in this situation?

14. I know other institutions advise against finding employment for those on the course; would you agree with that?

15. Does the intake of students truly reflect the rate at which retiring midwives leave the profession?

16. Regarding the non-midwifery placements; what areas are covered, and is there any option to choose specific areas of interest?

17. What teaching methods are used?

18. How do women respond to being cared for by students?

19. Do students where uniform while in the labs?

20. What's the age profile of a typical cohort?

Even if you don't want to use the above questions, you can use them to expand upon and create your own. It Is worthwhile preparing a question or two as it shows them you have prepared and have given serious thought to any questions you may need answering. Also you are there to interview them as much as they are you, you have to make sure it is the right university for you to commit too and spend three years studying there.

Your questions:

1...
....
....

2...
....
....

3...
....
....

4 SELECTION TESTS

The typical midwifery interview has evolved from just a 1-2-1 interview, as more often than not there are now other aspects involved such as a maths and literacy test to group discussions & activities. Most maths and literacy tests will last from 15-30 minutes. In most cases you will need to pass these to progress to a 1-2-1 interview.

Below are examples of tests you may be asked to undertake:

Literacy

The literacy test can be set out in various ways. You could be required to read some text and answer questions based upon the text or be given an essay title where you need to write an essay. Another option which seems to becoming more popular is the universities will give you an article or document and ask you to write an essay based on that. You may have one or the other or both, it will depend upon the university.

Example of a free writing task:

This scene shows people having a discussion:

Please write about a situation where you have had to lead or take part in a discussion, either at college or at work.

....

....

....

....

....

....

....

....

....

Example of a literacy (comprehension) activity one:

Please read the following text:

Coronary Heart Disease (CHD) still remains one of the leading causes of deaths in the UK (British Heart Foundation, 2009), with mortality rates significantly higher than in other comparable Western European countries. The burden of CHD falls disproportionately on people living in disadvantaged circumstances and on particular ethnic groups (Department of Health (DH) 2008). The prevalence of CHD in England rises markedly with deprivation: its incidence is 33% higher in men from the most deprived group compared with the least deprived group; in women it is at least 50% higher (British Heart Foundation, 2009b). However, the UK death rate for CHD has seen a gradual decline. A progress report estimated that the National Service Framework for CHD approach was saving more than 22,000 lives each year (DH 2007). Key achievements included: The reduction in deaths from cardiovascular disease for people <75 years of age by 40% was met five years early. The number of people suffering a heart attack who received thrombolysis within 60 minutes of a call for help increased from 24% of patients in early 2001 to almost 70% in 2007.

From: Jevon, P and Hodgkins, L. (2010) Nurse-led pharmacological stress testing: an overview. *British Journal of Nursing 19:9 569 - 574*

Write a short summary of the above in your own words. Please do not copy sentences directly. Please write a minimum of 4 and a maximum of 6 sentences.

....

....

....

....

....

....

....

....

....

....

....

....

....

....

....

....

....

....

....

....

....

....

....

....

....

....

....

....

....

Example of a literacy (comprehension) activity two:

Read the following passage and answer the questions which follow.

Titanic

In 1898 a struggling author concocted a novel about a fabulous Atlantic liner – far larger than had ever been built. He filled it with rich people and then wrecked it, one cold winters night, on an iceberg. Fourteen years later, a ship remarkably similar to the one in the novel was built by Harland and Wolff, in Belfast, for the British shipping company, the White Star Line. Both ships were about the same size and tonnage and could carry a similar number of people. Both had lifeboats for only a fraction of the passengers and crew and both ships were labelled as 'unsinkable.'

On the 10th April 1912, the real ship left Southampton on her maiden voyage to New York. On her way she, too, struck an iceberg and went down on a freezing April night. As the sea closed over the largest and most glamorous ship in the world with a list of passengers collectively worth, at the time, $250 million, the awful statistics of the tragedy were engraved on maritime history. Of the 2,206 passengers and crew, only 703 were saved. 65% of the passengers saved were First Class ticket holders. The ship had only half the number of lifeboats for the people she carried.
This White Star liner was the "Titanic." The ship in the novel was called the "Titan."

Put a ring round the letter which gives the most appropriate answer.

1. Which group of people were most likely to be saved from the Titanic?

    a. The best swimmers   b. The crew

    c. Passengers who paid the most for their tickets

    d. Women and children

2. What was the main contributing factor to the loss of life on both ships?

    a. They were both thought of as unsinkable

    b. It was a maiden voyage

    c. There were too many passengers on board

    d. There were insufficient lifeboats

3. There is a grammatical mistake on line 3. Should the word be changed to...

    a. winter's   b. winters'

4. In line 4 of the second paragraph, 'collectively' could be replaced by which of the following word or words?

    a. separately   b. individually

    c. in total   d. co-operatively

5. What was the name of the owners of the "Titanic?"

    a. Harland and Wolff

    b. A British shipping company

    c. The White Star Line

    d. A ship builder in Belfast

As mentioned you may be given an essay title where you need to write an essay on the day. You may not be given this title until the day or you may have been given it before hand and asked to prepare a reference list to take with you. Below are some examples of essay questions you may be asked:

1. All women should be offered a caesarean section – discuss.
2. Why do you think it is important to keep yourself healthy?
3. Why have you chosen this university?
4. What is the role of a midwife?
5. Explain your understanding of informed choice.

Using these essay titles, give your self 20 minutes on a timer and put pen to paper (pages are provided in this book). Write for each topic as if you were there at that interview day.

This is important because after you can examine your text for spelling and grammar errors, these exercises will also allow you to practice writing under pressure.

Essay activities:

All women should be offered a caesarean section – discuss.

....

....

....

....

....

....

....

....

....

....

....

....

....

....

....

....

....

....

....

....

....

....

....

Why do you think it is important to keep yourself healthy?

....

....

....

....

....

....

....

....

....

....

....

....

....

....

....

....

....

....

....

....

....

....

....

....

....

Why have you chosen this university?

....

....

....

....

....

....

....

....

....

....

....

....

....

....

....

....

....

....

....

....

....

....

....

....

....

....

....

What is the role of a midwife?

....

....

....

....

....

....

....

....

....

....

....

....

....

....

....

....

....

....

....

....

....

....

....

....

....

....

Explain your understanding of informed choice

....
....
....
....
....
....
....
....
....
....
....
....
....
....
....
....
....
....
....
....
....
....
....
....
....
....

To help interpret what the essay question may be asking when using words such as 'discuss' or 'explain' in the essay title. Below is a glossary which will help steer you into answering what they are asking. This is really handy to keep for when at university to help you decipher what essay questions are expecting from you.

Keyword	Definition
Account for	Give reasons for
Analyse	Identify essential features of a topic, separate it into its component parts and examine how they relate to each other, using research and evidence
Appraise/ assess	Estimate worth, importance and value
Clarify	Make a topic clear and understandable
Comment	Write about issues involved and give your own opinion
Compare	Show how two (or more) things are similar
Consider	Deliberate on and demonstrate the application of careful thought, using research and evidence
Contrast	Show how two (or more) things are different
Criticise	Write about positive and negative aspects of a topic stating your judgement. Support this with evidence
Define	Present concise, clear meanings which show what makes something different from other similar things
Demonstrate	Logically examine and provide evidence to support an argument to show understanding
Describe	Provide a detailed account of a topic

Discuss	Investigate or examine a subject by argument – give the pros and cons of points using research and evidence
Evaluate	Assess the worth, importance or usefulness of something using researched evidence to support your view
Examine	Investigate in detail, question and inspect the topic
Explain	Provide a clear account of a topic or give the reasons why something is so
Explore	Examine by working through systematically
Illustrate	Provide the main points, showing main structure rather than great detail
Interpret	Examine something and explain it in your own words
Justify	Give evidence which supports an argument or idea. Show why decisions or arguments were made, considering objections that others may make, using researched evidence
Outline	Provide the main points relevant to a given topic
Relate	Show similarities and connections between two (or more) things
State	Express briefly and clearly
Summarise	Concise account of main points
Trace	Follow development of something from its origin.

Helpful resources -

We recommend the following website to brush up your skills:
http://labspace.open.ac.uk/
You'll need to register (it is free) and then go to Skills and the top two links are full of resources for those who may have studied in Britain but not at degree level.

GCSE Bitesize is always another good place to revise :
http://www.bbc.co.uk/schools/gcsebitesize/english/ have a look at the reading and writing sections.

English Biz http://www.englishbiz.co.uk is another great resource which goes into a LOT of
detail, have a look at the "writing essays", "analysing non-fiction" and "grammar guide".

Mathematics

Maths tests will vary from university to university and nearly all if not everyone will do some form of maths test. This is due to them needing to know that you can undertake basic mathematics due to the nature of the profession (drug calculations etc.). Usually the maths papers will cover the following topics:

- Addition
- Subtraction
- Multiplication
- Expressing fractions as decimals
- Expressing figures as percentages
- Weight, volume and measures

Example maths questions:

1. **Solve the drug calculation:**

   A client is ordered 50 milligrams of Amitriptyline. 25 milligram tablets are available. How many tablets will you give?

   _____

2. **Solve the word problem:**

   Joel the local delivery man is preparing to deliver his parcels. His route has 48 drop zones with 90 parcels at each drop zone. Joel estimates that he will deliver all the parcels in 8 hours.

   a) How many parcels does Joel have in total? _____

   b) How many parcels will he have to deliver each hour? _____

3. Work out the following divisions:

a) 27 ÷ 3 =   b) 141 ÷ 3 =   c) 56 ÷ 7 =

4. Solve the drug calculation:

A client is ordered 30 milligrams of Frusemide intravenously. 10 milligrams in 1 millilitre of liquid for IV injection is available. How many millilitres will you administer?

_____

5. Use written methods to do long multiplication:

a)   55
     × 54
     ─────

b)   71
     × 66
     ─────

c)   191
     × 125
     ─────

_____   _____   _____

6. Use written methods to multiply whole numbers by a decimal:

Use written methods to divide a whole number by a decimal:

Raj bought 48 teddy bears at £8.95 each.

(a) Work out the total amount he paid.

(b) Raj sold all the teddy bears for a total of £696.

He sold each teddy bear for the same price.

Work out the price at which Raj sold each teddy bear.

_____

7. Use a written method to find a percentage of an amount:

In a sale, all the normal prices are reduced by 15%. The normal price of a suit is £ 145.

Ahmed buys the suit in the sale. Work out the sale price of the suit.

_____

8. Order decimals up to and including three decimal places:

Write these numbers in order of size. Start with the smallest number.

0.49; 0.5; 0.059; 0.59; 0.509

_____

9. Know some more difficult fraction/decimal/percentage equivalents, and use these to solve problems

(a) Express these numbers as decimals:

(i) 70%

(ii) 7/8

(iii) 1/3

_____

10. Use rounding methods to make estimates for simple calculations:

Juana walks 17 000 steps every day, on average.

She walks approximately 1 mile every 3 500 steps.

Work out an estimate for the average number of miles that Juana walks in one year.

_____

11. The following graph shows a journey:

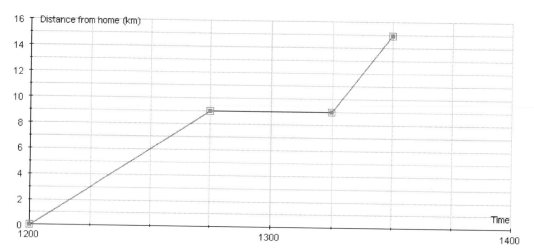

(a) How far was the cyclist from home after (i) 45 min (ii) 1 hr 15 min (iii) 1 hr 30 min?

(b) The cyclist's first stop was at Dorton.
   (i) How far is Dorton from the cyclist's home?
   (ii) For how long did he stop at Dorton?

(c) What was the cyclist's average speed
   (i) from home to Dorton?
   (ii) from Dorton to the end of his journey?

Write your answers:

a) (I)   (ii)   (iii)   b) (I)   (ii)   c) (I)   (ii)

12. Work out the following divisions:

a) $0 \div 5 =$ b) $45 \div 9 =$ c) $50 \div 3 =$

13. Work out the following fraction equations:

a) $\dfrac{1}{2} + \dfrac{1}{3} =$

b) $\dfrac{5}{7} - \dfrac{1}{4} =$

c) $\dfrac{4}{9} + \dfrac{2}{3} =$

14. Use written methods to do long multiplication:

a)
$$\begin{array}{r} 197 \\ \times \quad 2 \\ \hline \end{array}$$

b)
$$\begin{array}{r} 8629 \\ \times \quad 6 \\ \hline \end{array}$$

c)
$$\begin{array}{r} 9476 \\ \times \quad 8 \\ \hline \end{array}$$

15. Capital City is preparing for their annual winter festival. They plan to decorate their park with 129 strings of lights and each string of lights has 33 bulbs. It is expected to take 38 hours to decorate over the course of the week.

How many lights bulbs are there in all? _____

How many strings of lights are going to be hung each hour? _____

Helpful resources -

Maths Revision is a good resource http://www.mathsrevision.net/gcse/ that again covers most of the areas needed, you can even go more advanced up to A-level but you shouldn't need to for these tests as most of them are based on GCSE C grade questions.

GCSE Bitesize is always another good place to revise : http://www.bbc.co.uk/schools/gcsebitesize/maths/ I'd recommend you focus on the number section as that covers most of the areas stated previously.

Another site which is good for revision and free is Revision world http://www.revisionworld.co.uk/ click on GCSE, Maths and stick to the Number & Algebra section. This will cover the areas of maths that you need to revise.

Move on is also a good resource, scroll halfway down the page and you will see a list of numeracy tests available for you to download and practice with. http://www.move-on.org.uk/practicetestsResults.asp

Maths how to -

<u>Long multiplication</u>

When multiplying two numbers together, you must pay special attention to laying out the numbers correctly. For example, suppose you need to calculate 136 x 64.

This is how you should lay it out -
$$\times \quad \begin{array}{r} 136 \\ 64 \end{array}$$

Note that the longer number is placed above the shorter number. Also, the individual digits in each number are kept in their respective columns - thus, all units are in one column, all tens are a separate column, and so on. Finally, the 'x' symbol is placed well to the left, out of the way of the numbers. Keeping your working-out tidy when you are doing long multiplication will greatly help you avoid getting confused and making a mistake.

Multiplying two numbers

Here is a reminder of the steps involved in multiplying two numbers.

Multiply 257 by 46

1. Set out the calculation like this.

$$\times \quad \begin{array}{r} 257 \\ 46 \end{array}$$

2. Multiply the first number by the units digit 6.

$$\times \quad \begin{array}{r} 257 \\ 46 \\ \hline 1542 \end{array}$$

3. Now, look at the tens value in 46.

4. Remember that the 4 actually represents 40, so put a 0 under the 2 in 1542.

```
      257
  ×    46
  ───────
     1542
        0
```

5. Now, working to the left of the zero, multiply 257 by 4.

```
      257
  ×    46
  ───────
     1542
    10280
```

6. The multiplication is finished, so rule off and add the two numbers.

```
      257
  ×    46
  ───────
     1542
    10280
  ───────
    11822
  ═══════
```

7. So, 257 x 46 = 11822

Long division

A long division calculation is laid out as follows:

The number being divided is called 'the **dividend**' and it goes below the line, whilst the number being divided into the dividend (called 'the **divisor**') goes to the left of the bracket. Your answer, which is built up a digit at a time, goes above the line.

Dividing two numbers

Here is a reminder of the steps involved in dividing two numbers.

Divide 741 by 12

1. 741 is the dividend and 12 is the divisor, so set out the calculation like this.

$$12\overline{)741}$$

2. Divide 12 into 7. It does not divide.

3. Divide 12 into 74.

4. It goes 6 times (6 ÷ 12 = 72). Write 6 above the line over the 4, put 72 below 74, rule   off and calculate the difference, 2.

```
      6
12)741
   72   ← This is 6 × 12
    2
```

5. Bring down the 1, making 21.

```
        6
12)741
     72
     21
```

6. Divide 12 into 21.

7. It goes once (1 ÷ 12 = 12). Write 1 above the line, put 12 below 21, rule off and   calculate the difference, 9.

```
      61
12)741
     72
     21
     12   ← This is 1 × 12
      9
```

8. There are no more digits to be brought down, so the calculation is finished.

9. So, 741 ÷ 12 = 61 remainder 9

Group discussions

Group discussions and activities allow interviewers to assess your communication skills and see how you interact with your peers.

What are they looking for? The majority of the time you'll be observed on the following:

Leadership qualities

Ability to take leadership roles and ability to lead, inspire and carry the team along to help   them achieve group's objectives.

- A good leader will be able to initiate the discussion.

- She will also be able to contribute significantly and intervene when required.

- Giving the discussion a positive direction is very crucial.

- A good leader is also a good team player. Be cooperative, understanding and appreciative.

Example: To be able to initiate the group discussion, or to be able to guide the group especially when the discussion begins losing relevance or try to encourage all members to participate in the discussion.

Ability to reason

Ability to analyze and persuade others to see the problem from multiple perspectives without hurting the group members.
Example: While appreciating someone else's point of view, you should be able to effectively communicate your view without overtly hurting the other person.

Communication skills & body language

The participating candidates will be assessed in terms of clarity of thought, expression and aptness of language. One key aspect is listening. It indicates a willingness to accommodate   others views.

- Every applicant represents the university hence communication skills and body language command great importance.

- Dress well and be polite.

- Be expressive and firm to create an impact. However, do not be rude. Be sure of what you say and phrase your sentences carefully.

- Do not beat around the bush or talk about irrelevant things. Also note   that a good communicator is also a good listener. Let others speak and do not interrupt. If you have an objection, wait for them to complete and then raise it.

- Make enough eye contact to seem interested and serious; do not stare. Talk to your team members, not the evaluators. Remember, eyes are a big give away.

Example: To be able to use simple language and explain concepts clearly so that it is easily understood by all. You actually get negative marks for using esoteric jargons in an attempt to show-off your knowledge.

Interpersonal skills

Is reflected in the ability of the individual to interact with other members of the group in a brief situation. Emotional maturity and balance promotes good interpersonal relationships. The person has to be more people centric and less self-centered.
Example: To remain cool even when someone provokes you by with personal comment, ability to remain objective, ability to empathize, non-threatening and more of a team player.

Knowledge

Awareness is very important to do well in a discussion. Topics can be related to political scenarios, social consequences, your opinion of a particular person etc. You may be a brilliant speaker but if the topic is alien to you, you will be helpless.

Problem solving skills

Ability to come out with divergent and offbeat solutions and use one's own creativity.
Example: While thinking of solutions, don't be afraid to think of novel solutions. This is a high- risk high-return strategy.

More info:

Read the paper everyday/midwifery journals and keep up to date with relevant news topics. This will allow you to keep abreast with the latest and you will be confident about your points.

Speaking in front of people can be hard but you seriously need to get involved.. Make sure you take the points above and use them to your advantage, add to the conversation and bring a new view point. If someone is sitting not saying anything, throw the conversation open to them and draw them in, you've given them a lifeline but also demonstrated leadership skills!

Helpful resources -

English leap has some very good pointers on how to interact within a group discussion most of what is on this page is relevant - http://www.englishleap.com/career-resources/group-discussion-gd-tips-2

Get an idea of what is expected and how you can prepare. http://www.psychometricinstitute.co.uk/Psychometric-Guide/Assessment-Centre-Guide/Group-Discussion-Excercises-Guide.html

How is Evaluation Done In Group Discussions? http://placementsindia.blogspot.co.uk/2006/09/evaluation.html

5 TEST ANSWERS

Literacy (comprehension) activity two **answers**:

1. Which group of people were most likely to be saved from the Titanic?

    a. The best swimmers   b. The crew

    c. Passengers who paid the most for their tickets

    d. Women and children

2. What was the main contributing factor to the loss of life on both ships?

    a. They were both thought of as unsinkable

    b. It was a maiden voyage

    c. There were too many passengers on board

    d. There were insufficient lifeboats

3. There is a grammatical mistake on line 3. Should the word be changed to...

    a. winter's   b. winters'

4. In line 4 of the second paragraph, 'collectively' could be replaced by which of the following word or words?

a. separately

b. individually

c. in total

d. co-operatively

5. What was the name of the owners of the "Titanic?"

a. Harland and Wolff

b. A British shipping company

c. The White Star Line

d. A ship builder in Belfast

Mathematics **answers:**

1. 2

2. a) 4320   b) 540

3. a) 9   b) 47   c) 8

4. 3

5. a) 2970   b) 4686 c) 23875

6. a) £429.60   b) £14.50

7. £123.25

8. 0.059; 0.49; 0.5; 0.509; 0.59

9. (a) Express these numbers as decimals:

    (i) 70% = 0.7 (ii) 7/8 = 0.875   (iii) 1/3 = 0.3˙3 or 0.˙3

10. 1800 miles, 1900 miles, or 2 000 miles

11. (a) (i) 9 km (ii) 9 km (iii) 15 km (b) (i) 9 km (ii) 30 min (c) (i) 12 k/h
    (ii) 24 k/h

12. a) 0   b) 5   c) 16 r2 / 16.66

13. a) $\dfrac{5}{6}$ b) $\dfrac{13}{28}$ c) $1\ \dfrac{1}{9}$

14. a)
$$\begin{array}{r} 197 \\ \times\ \underline{2} \\ \underline{394} \end{array}$$
b)
$$\begin{array}{r} 8629 \\ \times\ \underline{6} \\ \underline{51774} \end{array}$$
c)
$$\begin{array}{r} 9476 \\ \times\ \underline{8} \\ \underline{75808} \end{array}$$

15. How many lights bulbs are there in all? _4257_____

How many lights are going to be hung each hour? ___3.39___

Printed in Great Britain
by Amazon